LODE

'*Lode* speaks to our confused and chaotic age. [...] In times of noise and bluster, Allnutt makes space for beauty.' – GRAEME RICHARDSON, *The Sunday Times* (Poetry Books of the Year 2025)

'Gillian Allnutt's 10th collection, *Lode*, plays with time and memory in works that feel prayer-like in their intimacy and simplicity...' – RISHI DASTIDAR, *The Guardian* (The best poetry books of 2025)

'...plain speech made devastating. [...] Allnutt's poems move between playfulness and austerity, eccentricity and anonymity. [...] this latest book may yet make her a lodestar for more readers, if they find their way to it. They should.' – JEREMY WIKELEY, *The Telegraph* (Poetry Book of the Month)

'There's no better poet alive in England, and no better poet of England, either. [...] Allnutt's poetry is lovely, strange and wise. These are profound and beautiful meditations on ordinary lives and the miracle of everyday language.' – VICTORIA MOUL, *Times Literary Supplement*

'Constraint and freedom, protection and danger – in *Lode*, Allnutt brings the full force of history to bear upon the words she weighs and, under these pressures, she holds diamonds in her hands. [...] There is plenty of white space in *Lode*, but one does not have to dig too far beneath its surface to strike magnetite, and then the forces of attraction pull everything together. *Lode* looks small – but it's huge.' – JOHN FIELD, T.S. Eliot Prize Reviewer

'Gillian Allnutt is humble, minimal: her quiet work has often gone unnoticed by contemporary town-criers [...] here we find God, small things, anchoritic loneness, history, the North; and a simple, firm poetic texture, short lines and glinting abstractions in strawbeds of solidity.' – CAMILLE RALPHS, *The Tablet*

'A quietly boundless collection that confirms Allnutt as one of the best English poets writing today.' – MARY ANNE CLARKE, *The Little Review*

Gillian Allnutt was born in London but spent half her childhood in Newcastle upon Tyne. In 1988 she returned to live in the North East. Before that, she read Philosophy and English at Cambridge, and then spent the next 17 years living mostly in London. From 1983 to 1988 she was poetry editor of *City Limits* magazine. Her collections *Nantucket and the Angel* and *Lintel* were both shortlisted for the T.S. Eliot Prize. Poems from these collections are included in her Bloodaxe retrospective *How the Bicycle Shone: New & Selected Poems* (2007), which draws on six published books plus a new collection, *Wolf Light*, and was a Poetry Book Society Special Commendation. Her most recent collections, all from Bloodaxe, are *indwelling* (2013), *wake* (2018), and *lode* (2025), her third collection to be shortlisted for the T.S. Eliot Prize. She has also published *Berthing: A Poetry Workbook* (NEC/Virago, 1991), and was co-editor of *The New British Poetry* (Paladin, 1988).

From 2001 to 2003 she held a Royal Literary Fund Fellowship at Newcastle and Leeds Universities. She won the Northern Rock Foundation Writer's Award in 2005 and received a Cholmondeley Award in 2010. Since 1983 she has taught creative writing in a variety of contexts, mainly in adult education and as a writer in schools. In 2009-10 she held a writing residency with The Medical Foundation for the Care of Victims of Torture (now Freedom From Torture) in the North East, working with asylum seekers in Newcastle and Stockton. In 2013-14 she taught creative writing to undergraduates on the Poetry and Poetics course in the English Department of Durham University. She lives in Co. Durham. Gillian Allnutt was awarded The Queen's Gold Medal for Poetry 2016. The Medal is awarded for excellence in poetry, and was presented to Gillian Allnutt by HM Queen Elizabeth in 2017.

GILLIAN ALLNUTT
LODE

BLOODAXE BOOKS

Copyright © Gillian Allnutt 2025

ISBN: 978 1 78037 745 2

First published 2025 by
Bloodaxe Books Ltd,
Eastburn,
South Park,
Hexham,
Northumberland NE46 1BS.

www.bloodaxebooks.com
For further information about Bloodaxe titles
please visit our website and join our mailing list
or write to the above address for a catalogue.

LEGAL NOTICE

All rights reserved. No part of this book may be used or
reproduced, stored in a retrieval system, or transmitted
in any form, or by any means, electronic, mechanical,
photocopying, recording or otherwise, without prior written
permission from Bloodaxe Books Ltd.

Requests to publish work from this book
must be sent to Bloodaxe Books Ltd.

Gillian Allnutt has asserted her right under
Section 77 of the Copyright, Designs and Patents Act 1988
to be identified as the author of this work.

Cover design: Neil Astley & Pamela Robertson-Pearce.

Digital reprint of the 2025 Bloodaxe Books edition.

Lost

Man with a garden
gate under his arm
wandering out of Eden

For Tom Midgley

*who took the garden gate off its hinges and didn't know
where to put it for the time being*

ACKNOWLEDGEMENTS

Several poems here were first published, in print and/or online, by the arts magazine *Monk*.

'Trist' was included in *All Keyboards Are Legitimate: Versions of Jules Laforgue*, edited by Suzannah V. Evans (Guillemot Press, 2023).

'Roughage' was included in *Shape-Shifter: a tribute to Gavin Selerie* (Shearsman Books, 2022).

'The way she remembered it' was commissioned by the BBC for Radio 2's Good Friday Special, *At the Foot of the Cross*, broadcast on Friday 2nd April 2021.

'The Song of Arachnid' was written and performed as part of The Festival of Minerva which took place in Hardwick Park, Sedgefield, in March 2022 and March 2023. The Festival was conceived and produced by composer and interdisciplinary artist Ed Carter and commissioned by Durham County Council.

'refugee born London 1949' was commissioned by Caroline Beck for *The Moon Under Water*, a series of podcasts about Weardale made in conjunction with Durham Book Festival and Northern Heartlands in 2018.

I'd like to thank Carol Ann Duffy and the Manchester Poetry Library for creating the on-line covid pandemic poetry archive *Write Where We Are Now*. The archive will remain as a collective record of poems written in that strange and difficult time and be available to future generations. At the time it was invaluable to me as an immediate destination for new poems and a way of staying in touch with the UK poetry community during the isolation of lockdown. Several poems here were first published in the archive in 2020.

I'd also like to remember my friend Diane Haigh (1949-2022) who, at the beginning of lockdown in 2020, set up *What To Do Today*, an experimental on-line Creative Studio providing courses on a variety of subjects, with groups meeting weekly on Zoom. She invited me to run a poetry creative writing course and, through that, brought both structure and stimulus to my lockdown life – and ensured that not a few of the poems here got written along the way!

CONTENTS

POSTWAR
12   Audience
13   Corbridge
14   refugee born London 1949
15   Dunstanburgh
16   a place beyond belief
17   Berthe
18   Crabapple moon
19   Poem for John Clinging
20   Pink Jenkins
21   Private Passion
22   Flame-thrower
24   My father, mislaid
25   note

LOCKDOWN
28   Golden Saxifrage
29   On having to leave York University without the clock
30   Azuma Meditation
31   The Walk (allowed)
32   If these days should be final
33   My Garden in Esh Winning
34   Lockdown
35   The way she remembered it
37   To be honest
38   At 71
39   Marney's Boots
40   Mask

EARTH-HOARD
42   'Wouldst thou witten thy Lord's meaning in this thing?'
43   At Ware
44   Beechwood

45	of the trees in the wood by the old pit line
46	summertime
47	Germander Speedwell *Veronica chamaedrys* (Linn.)
48	Do the birds worry?
49	Solitude
50	The Song of Arachnid
51	My hands, yes
52	*I love this poor earth for I have known no other*
53	Trist
54	dark night of the soul
55	Footnote
56	Afternoon in the Garden
57	Found Poem
58	Flâneur
59	for only then can
60	Sea Change
63	NOTES
71	Roughage

Lode

1 Orig., a course, a way, a journey. Later (*dial.*), a road, a lane.

2 Guidance.

3 A watercourse, a (natural or man-made) channel; an open drain in fenny districts.

4 A lodestone; *fig.* an object of attraction.

5 *Mining.* A vein of metal ore.

Lodestar

1 A star that serves as a guide for navigation etc., *esp.* the polestar.

2 *fig.* A person or thing on which one's attention or hopes are fixed; a guiding principle. Also an object of pursuit.

Lodestone

1 Magnetite that is naturally magnetised; a piece of this used as a magnet.

2 *fig.* A thing that is a focus of attention or attraction.

POSTWAR

Audience

Shyness, common and small,

a shrew, a plimsoll

and that's all.

The Queen, majestic, merciful,

the moon's own soul. Poor soul

must have acquainted herself with every holt and bolt-hole

of it, every last hat (optional).

Corbridge
(for my sister Elizabeth)

The river full of itself, intent, contained.

A listening in the rain
as if it were everyman or woman walking alone.

The church with its Roman arch carried straight
out of Corstopitum.

The tower grounded and squat as only the Anglo-Saxon.

The vicarage, the unforgiving, fortified as yet
for all the border-raids remembered
in its silent thick stone –

a brooding inwardness unfit
for man or beast.

By the king's oven we wait, as women do
as women medieval would have done
for bread or for the host –

involved in the recitation of the rain

involved in the recitation of our own
the told and the untold pain.

July 2017

refugee born London 1949

am no more stalled in God the story of God than you are whoever you are

have given it back to the void

with gratitude

out of the depths have I cried unto thee O Lord

the clock-tick loud in here

the some-of-it-Saxon tower

the stone Victorian stained glass more

and how without all that would I have come this far

my sorrow in war the story of war

my grandparents' war my parents' war

my parents' sorrow for

which will endure

as do the dour among these hills upheavals dark Satanic mills

before the war during the war after the war

we didn't know where we were

we didn't know who we were

delete etcetera

St Thomas's Church, Stanhope, Weardale
November 2018

Dunstanburgh

ARTHUR: Surliness sounds like the sea in waste places.

BETTY: You *would* say something like that.

ARTHUR: Wouldn't I – growing up by the North Sea there?

BETTY: Dunstanburgh. Egyncleugh. Lilburn, crooked bare tower.

ARTHUR: Aye, bare. Why did I take you up there?

BETTY: Precarious we were.

ARTHUR: *I* was. Too soon after the war.

BETTY: And you not entirely here, back here.

ARTHUR: In Blighty? I was nowhere.

BETTY: Dunstanburgh stood still.

ARTHUR: At the end of the Great Whin Sill.

BETTY: With its basalt soul.

ARTHUR: Before, during and after the war.

BETTY: The sea at the sheer cliff face for ever.

ARTHUR: Aye, for ever.

BETTY: Like Bert with his 'at it, at it, at it, at it, at it'.

ARTHUR: And I'd say 'Spit it out, lad!'

BETTY: And he never did.

a place beyond belief

tapping his fingers on the taut upholstered arm of the chair

as if it were abacus and he

preoccupied yet with the state of the world as it was

before the war –

rubbing the shine once more into the grain of table and sideboard
                                                                                       drawer

as if out of thin air

knowing all shall be mended or amended here

and she beyond fear –

in time the breaking of nations will come to pass

will pass

and a low wind also

through the garlic leaves and leaves of grass –

Berthe

And in the fading light of afternoon illiterate as stone

I heard the plough, horse-drawn, go up the field and down.

At last she'd lie among the modest shades she'd called her own –

old rose and sage and field-edge brown

the quiet embroidery of bodice, underbodice, done

for an English queen.

Crabapple moon

(to Clara, my niece)

Bring me my preserving-pan.
It belonged to Gran, *my* Gran.

Tip the washed crabapples in
and water they can boil and bob about in.

They'll simmer until tender
and *we* can wander.

We'll set two chairs upright in the dining-room
back to back with about six feet between them

and lay two tied-together bamboo poles
across the top. Think cross-bar on a bicycle.

We'll set the mixing-bowl upon the milking-stool
between-chairs, in the middle.

Bring me my jelly-bag. That's right, *that's* butter muslin.
Hold it open now and I will tip the tendered apples in,

suspend the bag from the bamboo poles and tie the corners over.
Quietly, under cover

of the coming night, we'll wait for it to drip into the mixing-bowl
upon the milking-stool

and all shall be well
and the moon and the heron, all manner of thing, shall be well.

Poem for John Clinging

Of you, John, there was nothing to go on –

nothing but your smithereen of skin and bone and plane.

You were one of *the quick and the dead*

and far too many of them to crowd into the dining-room.

You came alone, the chosen one

miscarried, made, laid out among them –

Gran, my mother and, in the blustering silence, Brodie Anderson.

And then you were no more alone, old navigator, party to

their incompletion.

So it was that when at last my mother helped me lay her down

I took you into my own heart's pondering

and still she claimed and wouldn't dream of claiming you her one and

only. 'You'd have liked him,' she said to me

often. I think I would have done.

Pink Jenkins
(for my father)

I'd love you in the long-shared anonymity

of day

undaunted, dear.

I'd love what was left of you after the war –

there was no other father

who would knock our silly heads together,

name Pink Jenkins for The War

Of Jenkins' Ear.

Private Passion
(for Tom)

While you were making the perch

for bird and bauble

to fly free from

I heard on the radio Bach

Erbarme dich

and what broke through

and what I fled

was all

of Sheol, unassimilable, whole

Christmas Eve, 2017

Flame-thrower

In memory of my father, Gordon Terry Allnutt, 1920-2006

Always the pudding burns with a ghost-blue flame.
Close to the walnut-shell, matchstick and cigarette-paper
boat, the work of a moment, the little tank
crosses the Christmas table, its destination secret,
its appearance perennial as that of the Christmas tree,
dear as the pasteboard palace

of Christmas Day. Again, again the Crystal Palace
burns in memory, in meltdown, all aflame –
he watches from the bathroom window still – among the trees
on Sydenham Hill. Later it will feel as if the world is tracing-paper
thin: the world before the war a secret
poste restante address, a palimpsest. And then the tank

rolls in, rolls on, and he must hunker down on Salisbury Plain. The tank
will sink almost, will fail to cross as if it were Buckingham Palace
on wheels or paddles. One of Churchill's own, it will turn back in secret
and set off again alone for Normandy, there to throw its lethal flame
on occupying troop and house and tree as if they were brown paper
troop, house, tree.

Now plump electric lights, like fruits, adorn the Christmas tree.
No candle. Now his daughters watch him clean the half-remembered tank-
fuel from beneath his fingernails. Before the meal he'll make newspaper
rolls to start the coal fire in the postwar palace
parlour, where the poker with its ghost-blue flame
plugs in, whose provenance remains a secret.

Mornings, he'll converse in silence with the milkman's horse. The secret,
he says, is in the sumac tree,
as he fights with the vigorous root of it, the autumnal flame
of leaves in a London garden. He lies like a tank,
she knows, like a blanket: it's something to do with Buckingham Palace
or a battered hut called Belsen in the morning paper.

It won't lie flat – as a poem on tracing-paper,
as a plan or elevation of the architect's heart, his secret
palace,
as a tree
(seen in the plan as if from above, from an aeroplane or the turret of a tank)
lies flat in the *bocage* after the deluge of flame.

My father, mislaid
Northumberland, circa 1960

In silence somehow he would ask me to forgive his suffering –
the shambles stilled, the crying shame of it.

He'd have me shoulder – love, that was it.

As if he thought love would be larger than the leper in him.

As if he thought love would be able to caul, to cradle, the small
                                                                      child over
the river between himself and home.

As if there were asylum.

As if he thought that love, once lost, were something to be
sought, remote,
elusive as the almost mythological

Chillingham cattle he'd tell me about
of a Saturday morning spent among hills and always

within shout of Cheviot.

Later he'd say to me aloud: 'You've made your bed –
now lie on it.'

note
(for db)

thank you for the little pewter elephant

he is my heart's content

inlaid mislaid in me like a parent

part of the memory of my mother's brother's life unspent

he is christmas past and christmas present

patient as the little doors of advent

as the ancient of days invariant

LOCKDOWN

Golden Saxifrage
(for Marney Harris)

You show me Golden Saxifrage

on the path by the burn

near where the sewer comes in

with your magnifying glass discern

opposite leaves rather than

the more unusual alternate ones.

You send me notice of an online

Literature Festival from the living-room

of the world. And now I

remember when you wheeled your old electric mower

down the long back lane, turned in at my garden, to render me again

my reasonable lawn. Today

I gather the quick cut grass

encouraged by the canny lass

of your kindness

knowing the quietude of that late September afternoon

has lingered and will linger in me as the sun and I

go down.

On having to leave York University without the clock
(for Woei Yng Tan in Singapore)

Quelle heure est-il?
What time in school?

What lesson going on
and on?

Your round gold clock as splendid as the sun
languishes here in lockdown

dull
as a sunflower in its seed-hull

hidden till summer
ticking over

in self-isolation.
Your clock is alone

and bored as a lady-in-waiting
biding

her time with her wooden beads
her worry-beads

keeping her counsel with care
until coronavirus is over.

Quelle heure est-il?
What time in school?

Azuma Meditation
(for Jane Wilcockson)

Only connect, communicate

courtesy of Zoom –

just as we are, we say, as if we were at home.

We bring the severed silence of the heart –

from Washington, Lartington, Langley Moor,

Esh, Esh Winning and Lanchester –

to this half hour, as if it were

the silence of eggs, a basketful

of eggs or toilet rolls.

And when we met before, all closeted

together in your attic of a Monday night,

did we communicate, connect?

What did we gain or lose when we listened instead

to the breathing of trains – *azuma, azuma* –

paused on the viaduct?

April 2020

The walk (allowed)

First lambs in the field on the far side of the hill.

Here I am stilled, no longer held

by the host and hostelry of world

too much with me.

I would not touch eyes, nose, mouth, the vulnerable

stile-post of the soul (supposed)

or earth at all –

though the hills are my familiars, call to me, call

as to the lambs. The light, alert

and growing –

March 2020

If these days should be final

let them be emptied of all

but lark-lift, the barely perceptible

heft of air among far mill-sails

and, here, the unassuming meanwhile

of Esh Hall.

April 2020

My Garden in Esh Winning

The sheep are loud about their lambs
and no cars come.
It's tea-time
in the small eternity of lockdown.

Nor does the tractor come
in no uncertain terms
of trundle-clatter.
Nor do trucks come

shifting down a gear
near the bottom of the garden.

Under the willow – whose would-be umbrella's
no stay against the stall and shove of the wind –
there's little protection from
Hargreaves.co.uk.

I lay my hand on the deeply divided
trunk of the willow, as if
patience had been tested there
and trust.

My hands are full of their own
sore places.

I hark at the thorn-pierced places –
blackthorn, hawthorn, rose-thorn –
of a garden weather-hardened,
cruel as time.

May 2020

Lockdown

Meanwhile

in the wait and see of every morning every day

le moment musical

for flute or oboe –

I said to my soul, be still, and wait

for sackbut or for viol

for silence buried in a bought field

held the while

as hoard unheard

unheard of –

or in trance

beheld

as wherewithal

the soul's

acknowledgement and song

of being

beholden to the earth –

an obol's worth.

The way she remembered it

While the king sitteth at his table,
My spikenard sendeth forth the smell thereof.
Song of Songs 1:12-14

I don't know what possessed me then. It was as if the moon
in Bethany, the alabaster moon, full moon, fell into my arms,
I being the one who was to take it to him.

How its clear white light burned through and through me then.
I wondered, were there really seven demons?
That was 'once upon a time'

and he was later, later on and he was come to us and Lazarus
sat at table with him. Martha, chided by him for her carefulness,
served them as always.

I, being left alone, bethought me of the alabaster box
in Mother's room: its pound of ointment, nard, spikenard, expensive
as love.

And so I brought it out, as if it were the moon,
into the dining-room and brake the box
before them and anointed him, his feet, road-worn.

Then with my hair I wiped them for I'd come
sudden, soon, with neither cloth nor clout upon my arm.
Judas Iscariot, there among them –

Almost I felt for him as he complained about my wastefulness.
Three hundred pence the poor, himself, would not again –
His poverty – his own, a poverty

of being in him –
was bare as bone or abacus set up within
himself, the meanest of men.

Then said Jesus, 'Let her alone:
against the day of my burying hath she kept this.'
And with those words, with none

he held me there, as I had held the moon, held
me in being, the deepest being,
showing me myself

anon
letting me come into my own
where, sudden, soon, I knew I'd always been.

To be honest

Truth is the ash they had to cut down at Flass Hall
Whose black uncompromising bud would not and never will be at
                                                              our beck and call.

Truth – as we, foolish, applaud with saucepan and wooden spoon –
Is the ambulance standing alone in the back lane.

At 71

I had never been offered the taste of my own mortality.

I was as yet in Blighty.

I asked them in imagination then –

By whom I mean the King of the World and the Queen –

Would they allow me to go on

Into the latitudes of alone

Into the anon –

And I, my heart, yet part of the penultimate?

Marney's Boots

They've forgotten what colour they were when they were born.

For fifteen years they've waited to be worn.

Now I will wear them into themselves.

But what colour are they when they're alone?

Are they neutral? Light tan? Brown?

These, with Dubbin, comprise my whole polish collection.

Wait. There is *Propert's Specially Prepared Leather and Saddle Soap*
                                                                to come.

Which I will consider before we go on.

It, lurking there in its tin, is a shrunken small bowl of tuppeny brown

Nestling its little rag of chamois leather in its lap.

With it I'll lather them back into being. Let them recover their confidence

Call themselves harness or luggage or car upholstery brown.

As it says on the tin.

Mask
(for Tom)

I am clout cast and caught in undergrowth
or lying dead mid-path, among middens, lost
in mud for good or gallimaufry. Look now –
I was well-intentioned. Worn with love
I would caress your face as if with kisses subtle
slow as silk or celanese. I'd cloud
your glasses quietly while in queues you stood
and waited for an ambulance or amber from the Baltic Sea –
simple, silly as the summer day
when Satan fell fine-fettled from the sky.

EARTH-HOARD

'Wouldst thou witten thy Lord's meaning in this thing?'

Unself-aware, un-

witting as the flower of winter

jasmine, listen –

At Ware

Chaste, thou art.

Green grow the rushes O

the grey-green willow.

Grace, the given way, of buddleia.

Nettled by knowledge art thou.

Gnarled, renewable, as if the heart

the river, now –

Beechwood

abiding in being, well-being.
Brood-hen

before the world's
stillborn

as word or byword, say, or
sobriquet.

To hart's tongue
home.

Illegible the stone
memorial to

men
who in the civil war – and alway

for the sake of one side or the other –
battled over Gloucester.

World of a sudden stilled in me
as if in meditation

and momentous
momentarily

without money
as I am.

July 2019
Edge, Gloucestershire

of the trees in the wood by the old pit line

surely they will not fall short of great-heartedness

giving the shawl and the shroud of their shade for us

they will cover us

sharing not sentiment but soil and soul with us

they will cover for us

bearing the brunt of light

they will shoulder the weight, the responsibility, of it

19 July 2022
Ragpath Wood, Esh Winning, Co. Durham

summertime

mute or musical as morning rain

and you as always gone

how I listen to your absence to my own

to the now and then of wood pigeon

its dear inconsequential circumlocution

Germander Speedwell   *Veronica chamaedrys* (Linn.)

Bright-eyed, upright, original Germander: do I really know you well?

Frail stalwart of the field, vernacular, you are, among many a synonym,

Fluellin the Male or *Veronique petit Chene*.

Twice gendered, then. For an earlier generation, though, as Gerard
would explain:

'*The Germander from the form of the leaves like unto small oak leaves,*

has the name chamaedrys given it, which signifieth a dwarf oak.'

But then, as Mrs Grieve would have it in her own plain words of 1931,

'*the likeness is not very pronounced.*'

Your glance is blue, lark-long, half-known, another ounce of song or rain.

Preoccupied, domestic as the chiff-chaff or the housewife

through the livelong day, you are – quicksilver, then, OK.

As Culpeper would say: '*It is a most prevalent herb of Mercury.*'

REFERENCE

Mrs M. Grieve: *A Modern Herbal* (first published by Jonathan Cape, 1931)

This includes the quote from John Gerard (1545-1612), author of *Herballe or Generalle Historie of Plantes* (first published, London 1597)

Nicholas Culpeper: *Culpeper's Complete Herbal* (first published, London 1653)

Do the birds worry?

Do the birds worry
where you have gone?
*We are all merry
in Babylon.*

Where are the icicles
once stave-long?
*Here they are melted
into song.*

Do you remember
the snow-covered lawns
where the birds scattered
peanut-skins,

where the unburied
bone
of day without further ado
began?

*Rather remember me
here in the Hanging
Gardens of Babylon,
bird-glad, unbelonging –*

Solitude

I invent the word *ditheridoo* and sit down.
This is my secret garden where I can walk and talk to myself without
                                                                            a mobile phone.
We owe it to one another to approach without expectation.
Who can ever be alone?
Even the columbine, like a little *corps de ballet* waiting in the wing of
Early afternoon, is poised to open.
Later the risen moon, as if mistakenly, will come upon
The Garden of Love in the middenstead of my own.

The Song of Arachnid

Webs are small and spacious as simplicity,
See-through as a summer's day, old-fashioned as
A slip of butter-muslin, girlhood's own, or
A cotton hanky.

We are poor predators, love to catch the light
As it falls from the air, invaluable as
What is not yet born, an acrobatic dot
And carry one. It's

Our Arachnid, ancestor, mother of all
Of us, mother of gorm and of gormlessness
Among women. Humble herself in origin,
Hard she works through us.

Nothing can cut the umbilical cord that
Calls us back to her, her bellyful of thread
Paid out and yet perpetual, her silken
Sac where we began.

She is alone, outwith the worn orb web of
The world. She's woven into the wherewithal
Of her own imagination, her mantle
Of maternity.

She is alone and she is loved among, as
No one else in all her anonymity.
One foot on the mountain, one foot on the web's
Her way, as she says.

My hands, yes

I have excommunicated them

for there is no more ceaselessness in them.

Yes, they are sitting comfortably

beneath the emptied udders of the moon

as women worn and washed and stained with transient dream

beyond the apple-tree of Eden.

Silent now the steppes of Central Asia where I once imagined them

as horsemen of apocalypse, of stone.

I love this poor earth for I have known no other

so mandelstam with nothing but his own *I am* would give it again

and again to each of us

anonymous

alone

in its brown paperbag

no longer stone

but bread bun

Trist

(after Jules Laforgue 'Complainte de l'Automne monotone')

the sun dead   everything abandons us   it is

unapprehended   lonely as God

how far away it feels

a low wind   poverty-stricken   needles

these convoys of martyrs burdened with their own importance
                                                              witness of

earth   so nourishing once   so to be trusted   *departed*

into [her] own country another way

abandoning us to our worn devices –

Autumn   *Season of mists and mellow*

dark night of the soul

after the river's reverie

there are interruptions to infinity

a tree   for example   will interpose itself

a tree borne up by the bank I builded here

alder say   or sycamore   whose sunk scabrous leaves

come-latelies   the pair of them   innumerate

nor yet knowing the number of their days

and who are you   in your peering into me impertinent   narcissus

sky   in an intermittent clouded-overing   obscures

infinity   and I am spared

sky   in a black hole or limbeck of ever-and-evering   unhalfbricking

all I considered my own   has left me

wondering   and if I am

9 October 2020
River Deerness, Esh Winning, Co. Durham

Footnote

Paul walks with Otis,

notices the river's broken

reverie, says –

Afternoon in the Garden

Joanne's Oscar – one short bark.

My own hand resting lightly on the new page of the notebook.

Wait.

A dip or ramp in the road the heavier vehicles balk at.

The dearth of air.

One bee working the wild geraniums for all they're worth.

Crow-caw.

24 June 2022
Esh Winning

Found Poem

There is no museum in Filamen.

We are a found people.

Evolved, we evolve with the wind.

Having no land, we leave all stones unturned.

We are the earth's, participant in, its poor inheritance.

Who can opt out of the indivisible dance of where and when?

We are momentary, dust.

We are neither first nor last.

We are absolved of our own imagination.

Flâneur

Consider

the nowhere in particular of air

as found abiding, biddable, wherein the seeded dream
or poem

may, with circumambulation,
be laid down

as if in some forgotten corner of a balcony –

au cinquième, say –

within the shaded kingdom come
of pansy or geranium

in some poor trough, some simeon, of earth
some shy repository of faith.

Consider the soul in ordinary
set free

from

home.

for only then can
(i.m. Di Haigh 1949-2022)

come broadcloth of light of fen of all that's

unconfined

by Gog Magog or anyone

when love itself liturgical co-opted or caught short

by thought in turn

of Ship of the Fen

of solitude or sequestration

lode or drain

by what is apt applicable well-meant

falls silent only then can

come the am that is and always is the same

the unknown known within

the common-law procedure of a poem

only then can

come the Small Blue butterfly's return

Sea Change

Put off the self-protective loneliness of God,

the pod, cast, of the word.

Put on the coat of calcium carbonate you'd wear

as pteropod or coccolithophore –

as if like them

you could become

Earth-hoard.

NOTES

NOTES

EPIGRAPH (9)
Definitions of 'lode', 'lodestar' and 'lodestone' are drawn from entries in *The New Shorter Oxford English Dictionary on Historical Principles*, edited by Lesley Brown. My edition was published in two volumes by Clarendon Press, Oxford, in 1993.

Audience (12)
I was awarded the Queen's Gold Medal for Poetry 2016 and went to Buckingham Palace to receive it from the Queen herself.

refugee born London 1949 (14)
Line 4 is from Psalm 130.

Poem for John Clinging (19)
My mother's brother John was the navigator in an RAF Lancaster bomber shot down over France in April 1943. The plane and its crew of seven exploded in the air. I knew him only as a photograph in a silver frame on the sideboard in my grandparents' house in South-east London. Brodie Anderson was my grandfather's name.

Pink Jenkins (20)
Pink Jenkins was a one-eared bear (the other was lost) made from an old pink curtain.
    The War of Jenkins' Ear was a conflict between Britain and Spain lasting from 1739 to 1748, mainly in New Granada and among the West Indies of the Caribbean Sea.

Private Passion (21)
Private Passions is a weekly music discussion programme on BBC Radio 3. Presented by the composer Michael Berkeley, it is Radio 3's equivalent of *Desert Island Discs*.
    Erbarme dich, mein Gott is an aria for alto and violin from Bach's *St Matthew Passion*. The words mean 'Have mercy Lord, my God, for the sake of my tears' and in the drama of

the Passion the aria reflects Peter's solitary heartache in the garden after he denies knowing Jesus three times.

Sheol in the Hebrew Bible is 'a place of still darkness which lies after death' (Wikipedia). It is the land of the dead rather than Hell. The definition of it has long been, and is still, something of a 'debatable land'.

Flame-thrower (22)
My father grew up in South-east London and, in November 1936, from the bathroom window of the family home, watched the Crystal Palace burn down. During the earlier years of WW2 he was training to become an architect, which was a reserved occupation, and so he was called up to the army only in time to train as part of the secret Overlord preparations for D-Day. He served as one of the crew of a flame-throwing tank. The ship conveying the tank had to be turned back in the rough weather of 6th June 1944 and attempt a second (successful) crossing a couple of days later. The Allies with their unwieldy combat vehicles and equipment struggled to clear the occupying German troops from the terrain of small fields enclosed by ditches and hedges on raised banks that constitutes the Normandy Bocage. In May 1945, some six weeks after Belsen was liberated, flame-throwing tanks took part in burning the remains of the camp to the ground.

My parents married in 1946 and my sisters and I were born between 1949 and 1954. We lived in a semi-detached house in South-east London. We had a gas-poker to start the coal fire that warmed the house in winter. We watched my father wash his hands very thoroughly before meals, guessing it might be a wartime habit acquired because of the tank fuel. We watched him cut back the sumac tree in the front garden as its roots destroyed the crazy-paving there. We watched him draw trees on architectural plans and failed to understand why they – seen as if from above – appeared as a circle of foliage with no trunk.

My father, mislaid (24)
In the 1960s Chillingham Castle and grounds were still privately owned. While it was possible to catch a glimpse of the herd

known as Chillingham Wild Cattle kept at large in the parkland, from one point or another in the surrounding countryside, I don't think we ever had the luck to do so. Now you can visit the castle; you can even book a place on a warden-led walk into the parkland to find the cattle grazing.

According to legend, Saint Christopher devoted his life to carrying the weak and poor across a river. One night, when he was carrying a child, he felt his burden grow heavier with each step. When questioned, the child declared that he was Christ and that Christopher was thus bearing the weight of the world.

Saint Francis of Assisi had a fear and abhorrence of lepers. One day, while riding his horse near Assisi, he met a man afflicted with leprosy. Though the sight of the leper filled him with horror and disgust, Francis got off his horse and kissed the leper and gave him money. Some accounts add that when Francis got back on his horse and looked around there was no one to be seen.

On having to leave York University without the clock (29)
When the first Covid lockdown was decreed in March 2020 I was doing a Royal Literary Fund Fellowship at York University. One of the students I worked with was Woei Yng Tan, a primary school teacher from Singapore taking time out to do a work-related PhD. She made me the gift of a clock – which I left behind when, suddenly, everything stopped for Covid and haven't been back to retrieve. Woei Yng returned to Singapore and, in spite of interruptions, eventually got her PhD.

Quelle heure est-il?: 'What time is it?'

Azuma Meditation (30)
Written after the first on-line meeting of the meditation group I was part of. Before Covid we met at a house near Durham station and would sometimes hear, breaking into the silence, the huffing and puffing of stationary trains. 'Azuma', borrowed for the name of a recent faster sort of train, is a Japanese word meaning 'East'.

My Garden in Esh Winning (33)
The road haulage company Hargreaves Transport Ltd occupies a large area of the industrial estate in Esh Winning, Co. Durham.

Lockdown (34)
[le] moment musical: 'This is one of the many terms introduced in the early nineteenth century, when pianoforte composition was being developed on the romantic side, as titles for short compositions for that instrument. It owes its introduction, apparently, to Schubert.' (*The Oxford Companion to Music*, ed. Percy A. Scholes, OUP London, 1942)

'*I said to my soul, be still, and wait*' is from T.S. Eliot's poem 'East Coker', *Four Quartets*.

'for silence buried in a bought field' in verse 4, line 1 refers to Matthew 13.44: 'Again the kingdom of heaven is like unto treasure hid in a field; the which when a man hath found, he hideth, and for joy thereof goeth and selleth all that he hath, and buyeth that field.'

The *obol* is known in Greek mythology as the fee paid to Charon, the ferryman of the underworld, who transported the shades of the dead across the river Styx or Acheron to Hades. His fee was a single obol placed in the mouth of the deceased upon burial.

The way she remembered it (35)
All four New Testament Gospels contain an account of the anointing of Jesus – at table during the festival of the Passover shortly before he was arrested and crucified – by Mary Magdalene. In his Easter sermons of 591 Pope Gregory I conflates Mary Magdalene with Mary of Bethany (sister of Martha and Lazarus) and with 'a woman in the city, which was a sinner'. Luke, at 8.1-3, refers to 'certain women, which had been healed of evil spirits and infirmities' and mentions 'Mary called Magdalene, out of whom went seven devils'. Apart from this last reference, and the mention of alabaster as the material of which the container of the ointment was made, I have relied on John 12.1-8 for details in the poem. Jesus's words spoken in verse 9 of the poem are a direct quotation from the Authorised Version of the Bible at John 12.7.

To be honest (37)
During lockdown we acquired the national habit of standing on the doorstep or in the street at 8 o'clock on a Thursday evening to honour the ('our') NHS for their courage and tireless dedication to work with applause and the making of a joyful sound on pots and pans and other unsuitable instruments.

At 71 (38)
Boris Johnson's sister has claimed that, when they were asked as children what they wanted to be, Boris replied 'King of the World!'

Marney's Boots (39)
A gift to myself during lockdown. They were around fifteen years old and barely worn.

'Wouldst thou witten thy Lord's meaning in this thing?' (42)
The title is a quotation from *Revelations of Divine Love* by Julian of Norwich, translated by Clifton Wolters and published in Penguin Classics, 1966.

Do the birds worry? (48)
The title of the poem is borrowed (with thanks) from that of a Ukrainian folk song.

It is unclear whether the Hanging Gardens of Babylon were an actual construction or a poetic creation (Wikipedia).

Solitude (49)
'The Garden of Love' is the title and subject of one of William Blake's *Songs of Experience*.

The Song of Arachnid (50)
In Greek and Roman mythology Arachne was a gifted young weaver of common stock and unusual reputation who challenged the goddess Minerva to a competition of perfection at the loom – and won! The goddess, outraged, demanded of Arachne that she acknowledge herself, Minerva, as the provenance of her gift. Arachne refused – whereupon Minerva tore Arachne's

piece of weaving, with its mocking portrayal of herself and fellow gods, from her rival's loom and set about beating her up. Arachne, in despair, tried to hang herself, but Minerva spared her from death by turning her into a spider for all eternity.

In this poem I imagine that in time Arachne became the leader of her tribe of spiders and eventually was deified as the goddess Arachnid. For centuries now and across the earth, the tribe has held an annual festival in her honour. The celebrations culminate in the singing of an Ode to her and to their own being in her. This is their Song of Arachnid.

The poem is spoken by an elder of the contemporary tribe who reflects upon the nature of the goddess and expresses gratitude both for the goddess herself and for the tribe's relationship with her.

I love this poor earth for I have known no other (52)
The title of this poem is a quotation from Russian poet Osip Mandelstam (1891-1938). I do not know the source of it.

Trist (53)
This is a version/translation of stanzas from the poem 'Complainte de l'Automne monotone' by French poet Jules Laforgue (1860-1887).

Quotations at lines 6/7 and line 9 are from Matthew 2,12 and Keats' 'To Autumn' respectively.

Footnote (55)
Otis is a dog.

Flâneur (58)
au cinquième: on the fifth floor

for only then can (59)
The Gog Magog Hills are a range of low chalk hills, extending for several miles to the south-east of Cambridge.

The Ship of the Fen is the local name for Ely Cathedral which can be seen across the Fens from miles around.

Lode: an open drain in fenny districts.

The Small Blue Butterfly: Conservation status: Protected in the UK under the Wildlife and Countryside Act, 1981. Priority Species under the UK Post-2010 Biodiversity Framework (www.wildlifetrusts.org).

Sea Change (60)
Pteropods are minute free-floating marine snails that make up the base of the oceanic food web. Like coccolithophores, they build themselves shells of calcium carbonate. (The current increasing acidification of the ocean is affecting these shells, thinning and damaging them.)

Around seventy million years ago what is now the south coast of England was submerged beneath a shallow sea. The sea bottom was made of a white mud formed from the fragments of coccoliths – the skeletons of tiny algae that lived in the surface waters of the sea. This mud became the chalk of which the White Cliffs of Dover are built.

Roughage

Gusts in grasses. Muster of

grass and ghost and graces.

World without edge.

EU DECLARATION OF GPSR CONFORMITY

Books published by Bloodaxe Books are identified by the EAN/ISBN printed above our address on the copyright page. This digital reprint was manufactured by Lightning Source at the printing works indicated in their code. This declaration of conformity is issued under the sole responsibility of the publisher, the object of declaration being each individual book produced in conformity with the relevant EU harmonisation legislation with no known hazards or warnings, and is made on behalf of Bloodaxe Books Ltd on 22 May 2025 by Neil Astley, Managing Director, editor@bloodaxebooks.com.

No part of this book may be used or reproduced in any manner for the purpose of training artificial intelligence technologies or systems. The publisher expressly reserves *Lode* from the text and data mining exception in accordance with European Parliament Directive (EU) 2019/790.

www.ingramcontent.com/pod-product-compliance
Lightning Source LLC
Chambersburg PA
CBHW061740070526
44585CB00024B/2757